Quick Bath, Long Bath

By Cameron Macintosh

I have a quick bath
in this pond!

I flap my long wings
and get wet.

My chicks swim with me.

The chicks' necks will be long when they are big.

But today, they are little.

Mum and I get in a big bath when it is hot.

When Mum gets out, she is wet.

She mops up the wet with muck!

This is such a hot bath!

My chum checks me
for bugs.

Then I have a long nap
in this hot bath,
which is fun!

I am in no rush.

My long bath is
in this thick mud!

Do you think that is odd?

I sit in the mud and then nap in the hot sun.

What a top bath!

CHECKING FOR MEANING

1. Who checks the monkey for bugs? *(Literal)*
2. What does the wild pig do after having a mud bath? *(Literal)*
3. Are animals' baths always about getting clean? *(Inferential)*

EXTENDING VOCABULARY

wings	What are wings? What types of animals have wings?
chum	Who is the chum in this text? What is another word that the author could have used instead of *chum*?
rush	What does the word *rush* mean? If you rush, are you moving quickly or slowly?

MOVING BEYOND THE TEXT

1. How are animal baths different from the baths that people have?
2. Monkey friends help each other by removing bugs from their fur. What do you and your friends do to help each other?
3. What are some other things that animals do in the wild?
4. Would you like to have a bath in mud? Why?

SPEED SOUNDS

PRACTICE WORDS

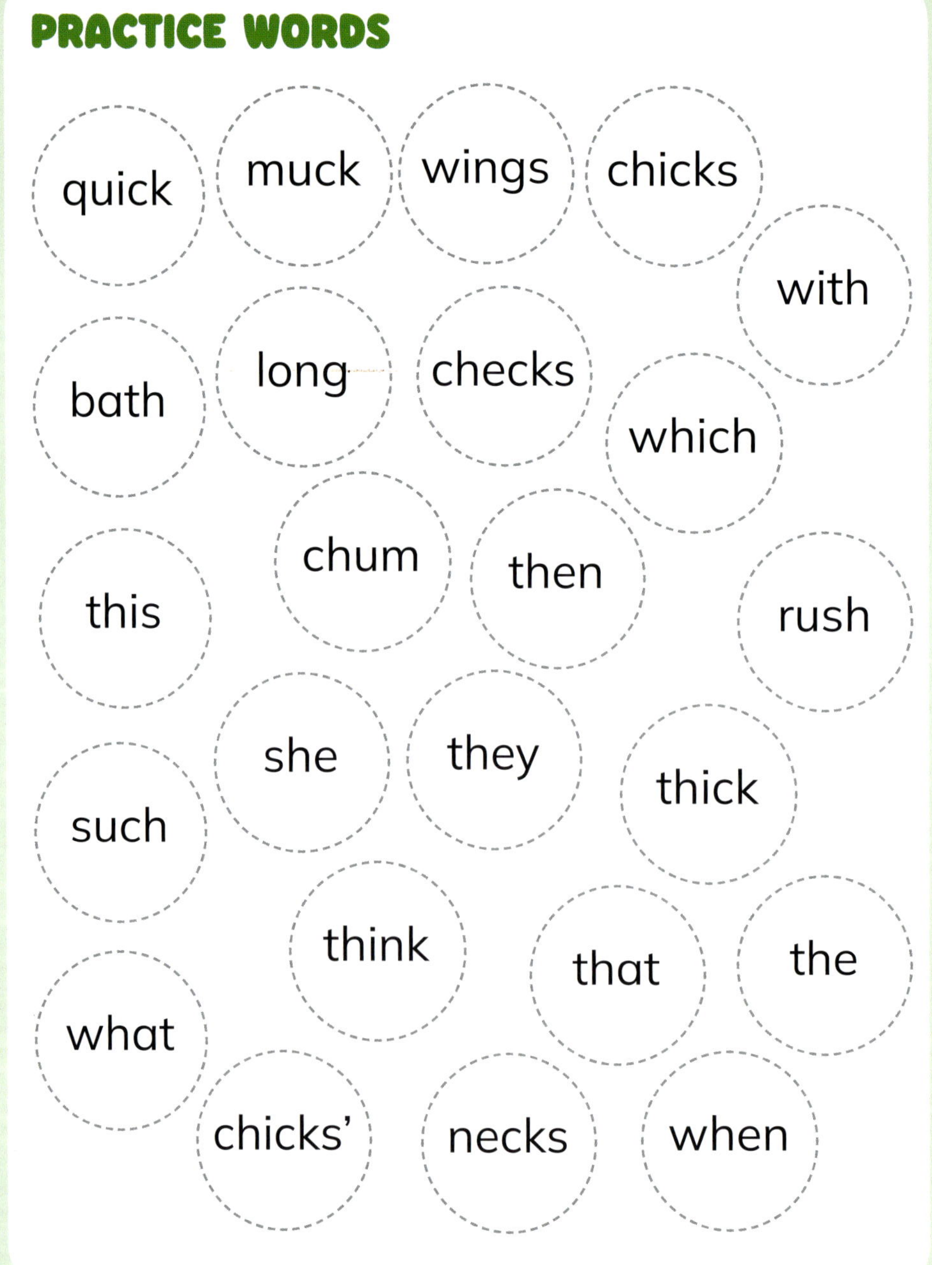